Pass Me By
Poems by K.B. Walker

Contact me

AuthorKBWalker.com

Facebook: K.B. Walker

Instagram: AuthorKBWalker

DEDICATION

To everyone that didn't believe in me, this is the outcome. To those that did, I cannot thank you enough.

CONTENTS

PART I: UNCERTAINITY

What's the Price? 1
Most Days 2
The Frame 3
Ideas 4
Flames 5
Pressure 6
The Maze 7
Resurrection 8
Dreams 9
Beauty Among Chaos 10
Confession 11
Cruel Perfection 12
Debt 13
Open Your Eyes 14
Voiceless Cheerleader 15
Finish Line 16
I Am 17
Ink My Fears 18
Wake Them Up 19
The Musician 20
When Words Come to Life 21
Method Memory 22
No U-turns 23
Lock & Key 24
Broken Ladder 25
Please Don't Pass Me By 26
Manual of Life 27
Bloom 28
Dying too Soon 29
First Snow 30
Broken Heart 31
Shame 32
Don't Look My Way 33
The Gatekeeper 34
The Seas 35
Open 36
Planting Flowers 37
Where Are You Going? 38
Night Vision 39
Concrete Feet 40
The Spirits 41
The Rollercoaster 42
The Scale 43

CONTENTS

PART II: REALIZATION

Writing Rituals 44
The Waters 45
For you 46
Golden Light 47
Waiting 48
The Waves 49
Thanks for the Hurt 50
Building 51
Call Accepted 52
The Murals 53
The Silence 54
Seasons 55
Unwanted Materials 56
It's Just Paper 57
The Lies 58
Clear View 59
Standards 60
Just Read Them 61
Stay 62
With Me 63
Reading Memories 64
New House 65
The Wheel 66
Constellations 67
Tribute 68
Stamps 69
Pass Me By 70

Part I

UNCERTAINTY

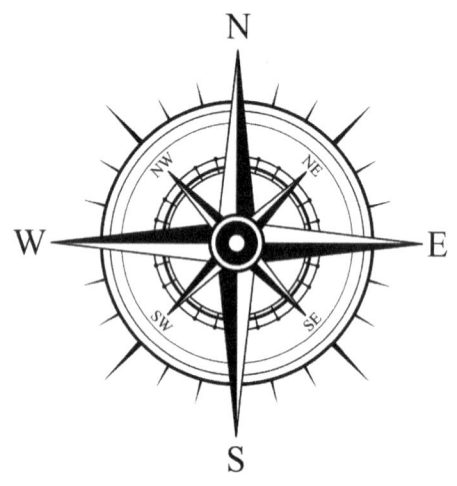

WHAT'S THE PRICE?

This road has no signs, I can't help but feel lost
Truly I cannot remember my life's start
Where's my future and how much does it cost?

Money crunches under my feet like frost
Hardening my already cold heart
This road has no signs, I can't help but feel lost

Each corner turned, a new bill for me is tossed
And with each step I'm being ripped apart
Where's my future and how much does it cost?

Is this a path I've already crossed?
Unsure when appropriate to turn and dart
This road has no signs, I can't help but feel lost

My legs are lead, I begin to exhaust
There's only so much worry that can fill my cart
Where's my future and how much does it cost?

By time I arrive, everything could be mossed
Further then from my freedom I would part
This road has no signs, I can't help but feel lost
Where's my future and how much does it cost?

How do I care for you
When most days
I cannot care for me

These days seem much harder
Than those once remembered
As you were growing
When you needed me most
I could not be there for me

How do I care for myself
When most days are spent
Missing my past

...most days

THE FRAME

Stuck in this frame of a mediocre life
Sinking deeper, swimming the sea of stagnant life

Friends and family, greeted with claims from death
Their full potential never seeing a mortal breath,

It's able to remember the shame from our past
We see truth behind the eyes of this labeled life,

I am nothing more but a game, played
Day-to-day for hours on end by a insomniac life lame ,

There will be a moment I am able to proclaim my power
Perhaps on Earth, or lit by a flames in a galactic hour.

I don't think my **ideas** are meant to escape
My mind
If I try to put them on paper
Drawn
Written
Painted
All turn into dark puddles
As they hit the page
As impure as we become
The minute we take our first breath
Sin comes quick

FLAMES

People always use the phrase
"All bark no bite"
Words will get you what you want,
Right?
Manipulative
Twisted
Envious
But I believe you're different
You have that fire
When it gets sparked,
There's no way to quickly extinguish
It burns slow and steady
Days and days and days
As for your bite
I hope it burns
Like their words
I hope their wounds ooze and fester
I hope they're left with scars
The same scars
Those words once put on you

PRESSURE

Pressured to feel whole
What they did not know
Was they were breaking me

I begged for some glue
To seal my cracks tight
Please make me whole again

I found damages are permanent
Below the surface

My porcelain skin
May heal, but
My heart will hurt
On each brand new day

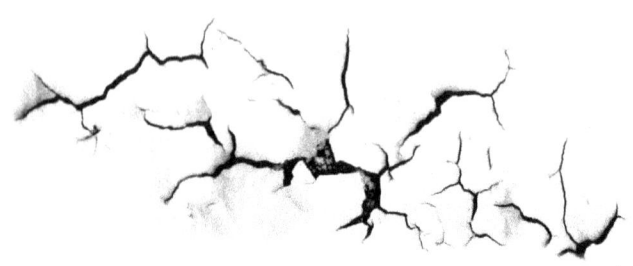

THE MAZE

My mind is nothing but a maze
Solitary confinement with whispers
Of my fears drifting by
The first I meet is self-doubt
The next, criticism
Lastly, and the worst,
A spinning sign
Of which path is right
How many walls are there?
How many of them did I put up?

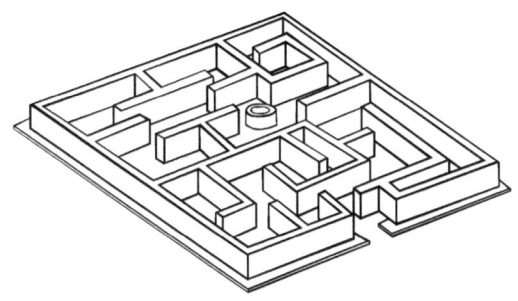

I don't know what killed me first:
the pressure to find success,
which felt as if there was little room to breathe,
drowning in my endless river of self-doubt,
or the fear to put everything aside
and chase my dreams.
I don't ponder how or why,
For I feel a resurrection coming
I have a new perspective each day
Soon, I will feel alive again.

                                    The **resurrection** is coming

My **dreams** reflect my fears
Usually I'm lost, trapped, looking
For a specific sign,
Only to be met with
Emptiness
I continue my search for what
Feels like days, with no luck
Of finding the way out

BEAUTY AMONG CHAOS

Navigation
Chaos
Finding your path
Maybe you never do
Searching for your purpose
Tick, tock
Better beat the clock of Death
Attempting to find fame
And you were never called back
Twists, turns
Hills to climb and cliffs to hang from
Find beauty in your chaos

<u>CONFESSION</u>

I must confess
I've been writing,
Drawing, creating
Since I could hold a crayon
If only I had known
What turmoil it would bring
A fight to be in control
As my uncertainty engulfs
Everything I've ever loved

CRUEL PERFECTION

It was beaten into my head that anything less
than one-hundred percent
was the epitome of failure.
I was supposed to be perfect
from the start in your eyes;
With no room for growth.
Now, I don't allow myself to make errors.
Why am I not perfect
if that's all
I was ever supposed to be?

Actively in **debt** to myself
For times I lost hiding myself
In the darkness
Infringing my own creative freedom
Because everything was never enough

OPEN YOUR EYES

Being receptive is not an easy thing. The idea of self will block out those gifted with wisdom.

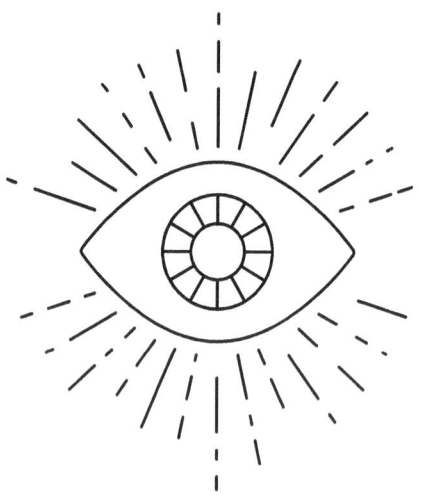

VOICELESS CHEERLEADER

Too often I've found myself focusing on the goals of those around me
I left mine behind to disintegrate while I nurture another's
I always believed
That you are your own biggest cheerleader,
It seems I lost my voice long ago

The decision to leave behind everything I knew
Lead me to the greatest journey of all
Two towns in two years
I can't tell you which means more
Friends, mentors, classmates,
All wiped clean from my slate
But not forgotten… really

Cherished now more than ever
New places, new people, shut down
Until the **finish line** was crossed
We did it together, though

New friends, new mentors,
New distant classmates
Where navigating this unknown
Is all we've known

I AM

No matter where
I AM
I find it hard to stand still
I AM
Afraid I will miss out
I AM
In need of constant change
I AM
Scared of a stagnant and mundane life
I AM
Driven to see everything possible
I AM
Unsure where my last stop will be
I AM
On a train to the unknown

INK MY FEARS

Why would I ever dream of exploiting myself on paper?
Inking my fears and uncertainties
Then leaving them closed on a dusty shelf
Just too far from the sun's reach
I hide between my sheets,
Hoping the dawn of criticism never comes,
The most important thing is
Everyone has seen
Evil
And maybe
My words can soothe a damaged soul
So, I'll keep writing for them

WAKE THEM UP

Crack the surface of those wandering this imperfect world
Release their souls' desires
Watch them come back to life
Since professional façade hardens us too quickly

THE MUSICIAN

We tumble into this world
With no prior demonstration on how to live
Walking into a studio and being expected to
Write a song with no prior knowledge of music

WHEN WORDS COME TO LIFE

I wish I could celebrate words
Have them feel my Love,
Go further with Encouragement,
And understanding Pain
I wish they felt what I feel with them

METHOD MEMORY

The method to fit in soon becomes a memory;
an allusion of the fake

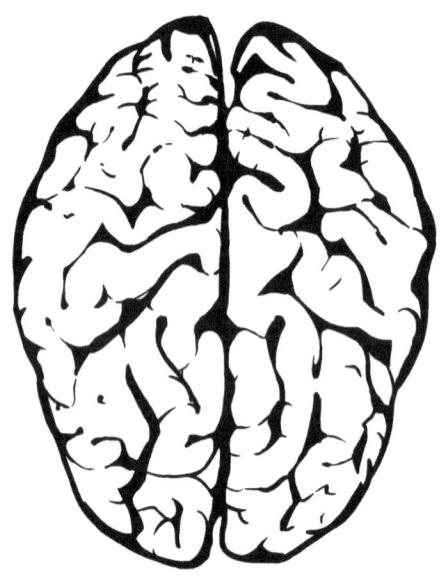

NO U-TURNS

Traveling this never-ending road we call life.
No signs, no arrows, no stops.
I think I've been going the wrong direction.

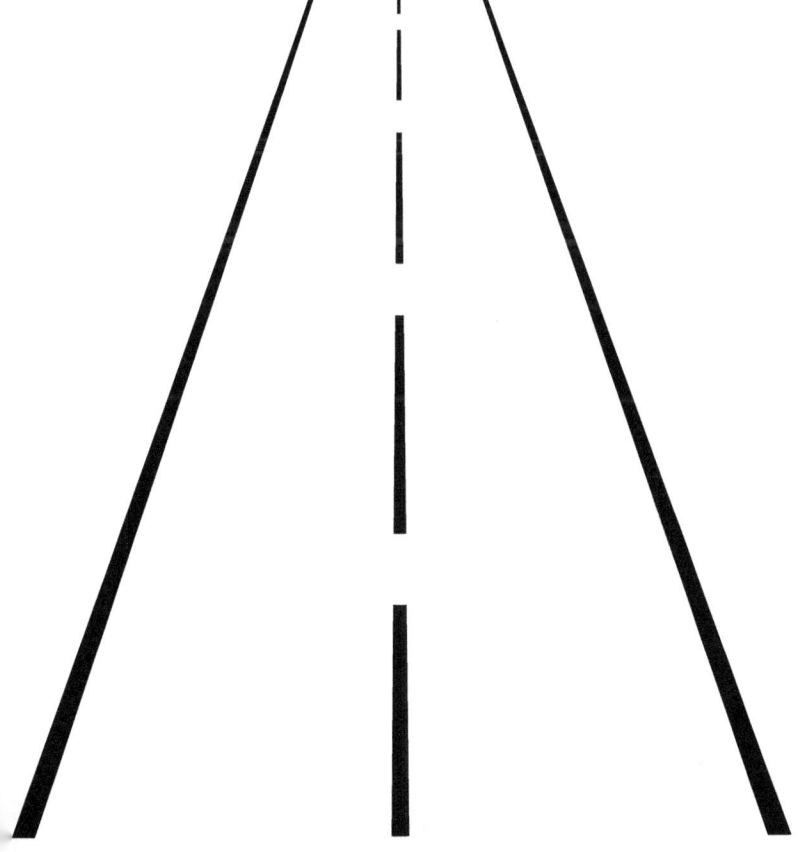

<u>LOCK & KEY</u>

Exhausted and ready to scream,
The words do not come naturally
I need to rest; so much left unsaid
These words follow me until they're set free
But I've seemed to lost my lock's key

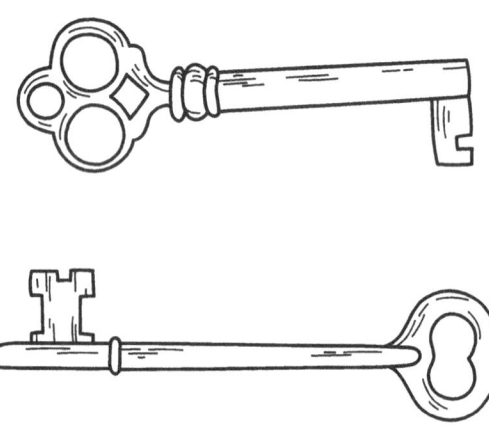

BROKEN LADDER

I feel as if I'm climbing
an infinite ladder
with missing rungs
Making the trip more strenuous
On and on
I grasp and pull
Hoping myself to the next safest point
I look forward in dread
Knowing this will never end
But
 I can't go back either.

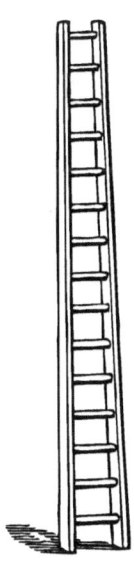

PLEASE DON'T PASS ME BY

I'm a flower
In a world with no bumblebees
Days on end I wait for one to stop and bury themselves in my petals
To take from me any golden wisdom their bodies can carry
In the weeds I'm left, almost asking to get picked
At this point, please don't pass me by

MANUAL OF LIFE

If I was given the chance to change my past,
I must admit
I don't think I would be any happier
There are a million other lives
I could have lived
None coming with a user's manual

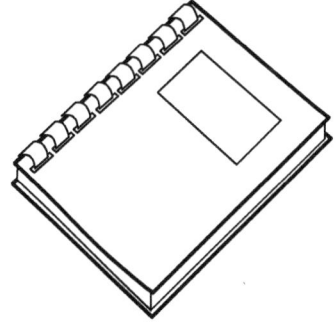

BLOOM

I was never the one
Finding success when desired
More like a camellia
saving its blooms 'til winter
Sharing its growth
when others need motivation most

A new fax of ideas
marching in at once
As if they're being hurried to simply exist,
Jaded before they reach paper
A false representation of creativity

                                                They're **dying too soon**

As uncertainty boils through me,
I still feel frozen in my works
My words stick slowly to the page
Like the **first snowfall**
My ideas concealed
In this block of ice with no insight
Of when the sun will thaw
all that has been antiquated

BROKEN HEART

The color of dawn brings anxiety from deep within me.
I want to feel pleasant in the beginning of a new day,
Instead I'm bewildered at the lack of work pumped
from last night's heart.

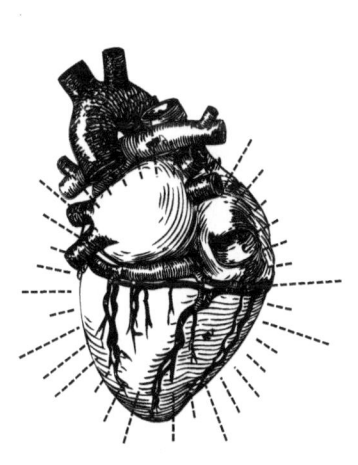

Invincible to the shame I bring upon myself,
For the results are inconclusive
I strap in and fight the lackadaisical
Version of myself

DON'T LOOK MY WAY

I distance myself from the ugly
Found walking among us
Trying to relax but I am brass
Forever and slowly tarnishing
from the toxins of today

THE GATEKEEPER

Too protective of my words
Like a gatekeeper
Restricting others as they stretch
Adamant to see what's beyond,
But I'm too concerned they'll find me strange

THE SEAS

Eyes surrounding me, drowning in resentful stares
As I try to fight my way to the water's surface
Waiting below are hands I wish to never hold
Their grip has me hostage from the clean air that has yet
to fill these fragile lungs
Floating, sinking deeper into the abyss of uncertainty

OPEN 24/7

I'm my own worst critic when my work should be something I'm always proud of.
The headquarters of my self-doubt: open seven days a week, with no desire to close its doors

PLANTING FLOWERS

I strew ideas like papers
crowding the surface of my desk
hoping to plant them about
A flowery display, bright and full of life.
This world is too cynical,
They would trample my flowers

WHERE ARE YOU GOING?

Bustling city streets and endless nights
I sit and watch the passerby
come and go with ease

I wonder what makes those steps worth it,
Is it someone they love or just mundane trod
to a home with empty words?

Is it a career that does more than make ends meet?
Are they escaping their problems
or mending a broken heart?

Their journeys much more intriguing than this one
that has yet to start

NIGHT VISION

This feels like striking matches,
just to watch them die out
before they fully light
Five, six of them gone to waste,
Mysteriously.
I've learned to see in the dark

New people to meet each day
 with numerous paths to stroll
It's hard to go far as the girl with **concrete feet**
Too heavy to launder with the others
I can only watch as they move forward

Chasing **the spirits** of my future into a hallway
Of only closed doors
But even my future self does not know which to open

THE ROLLERCOASTER

                                                                    up
                                                                  goes
                                                         only
I'm riding a rollercoaster that

So much suspense, with no chance of release

The scale teeters between fear and confidence,
baiting me:
Surrender into the temporary authority of emotion.
Can't indulge-
I combine the two and protest for my
end goal

Part II

REALIZATION

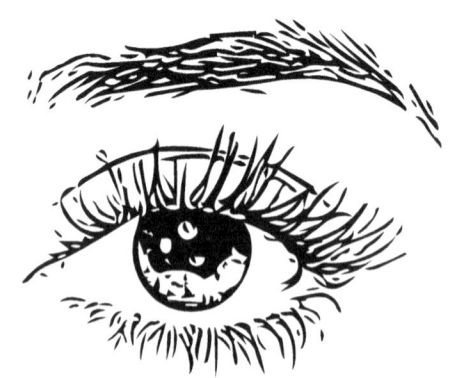

WRITING RITUALS

I see writing as one of the most
Sacred forms of art
For you can write of love
And share with those whose hearts
Beat the same rhythm
Of loss and loneliness
And vacuum yourself
Out of that never-ending void
Of depression
Perhaps you write of anger
And burn every paper
After you see that word
Can't be read through tear stains
Writing is not something you can do
Only when you feel like it
It must become your ritual

Split the water
Let me cleanse this weary body
Blood of those lost last
Will wash the fastest
Leaking from me, an ink-filled sponge
That cannot wring itself dry

Sing the song of renewal
Watch this temple of mine restore
Building stronger with each destruction
From days of instability to support
The winds now only rattle dust
From the willpower in this slowed heart

I will forever seek **these** waters.

<u>FOR YOU</u>

I wrote this for you
With all your beauty and flaws
Whether successful or struggling
I wrote this for you

On your earliest mornings and latest nights
Through your softest laughter and loudest cries
I wrote this for you
Hoping that you see

All the magic you have to bring
I wrote this for you
I hope you find inspiration
Strong enough to diminish fear

I wrote this for you
I hope you always remember
When no one seems to be there
I write this for **You**.

You can't keep waiting for opportunity to
find you
You can't allow your **golden light** to dim
To wither
You can't let this world go dark
Keep shining your light
those that need it most will
find you

WAITING

Too many things lost
Opportunities not taken
Words unsaid
Waiting for the "right" moment
Waited too long and only came to see
Any moment is the right moment
to show
what your soul is made of

To find my purpose at such a young age
would merely be a waste
A waste of flesh that doesn't
wearily search the world and discover it,
too, has imperfections
It would be boorish to be so well-planned,
to have such advantage at swimming
the sea of possibilities
To float past moments that would shape
me, to miss out on conversations with
those struggling to tread water,
To surpass those **waves** that beat me blue
Without it all, I wouldn't have these
words.

THANKS FOR THE HURT

Those that condemned me
Now must read the results
of their treatment.
Your words
only gave me
more to
write.

Brick by brick,
I'm building the life I want most
No matter the expense or
remodeling required
I will not be defeated
My work never incomplete
I obey the beckoning of labor
Who can build a home
for my inconsolable mind
better than I?

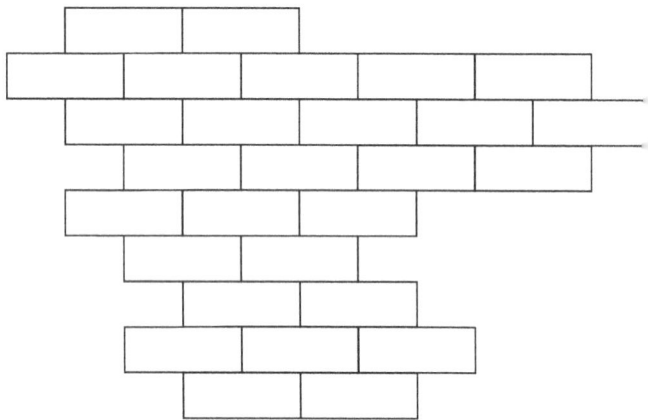

CALL ACCEPTED

I want what I say to be alluring,
Drawing in any wandering eyes
Letting them scale the words
to fit their own needs

I answer the voiceless calls
so they don't sit staring
at scars they've acquired
While seemly wishing to be heard.

We are dropped into this maze
The very moment we can walk.
As we go,
Greeting more twists and turns
More walls blocking
What I thought was right. After the time
Of feeling lost
I've learned to create **murals**
Along these barriers
Making beauty from the blank slates
In front of me
Instead of searching for the big picture
Painted by another artist.

I was once scared of silence
As it yelled I was alone
I may be the only body present
but I feel the Earth's love
And hear **the silence** of the stars
Keeping my mind entertained

SEASONS

This world would be faded
Without the art you bring to it
The trees would sadden
And flowers would wilt
Missing your beauty in every season

UNWANTED MATERIALS

It's not about the money
Or number of people that see
It's not about fame
Or having time to be free
It's not about the praise
Or words that keep me warm
It's not about the layout
Or the picking a form
It's not about material gains
Or things I can count
It is about me living
To the greatest amount

IT'S JUST PAPER

Whoever insists money
determines our worth
should find a new mantra.

One that is uplifting,
not cornering victims,
scaring them into acute paranoia.

All over something
that has minimal value at all.

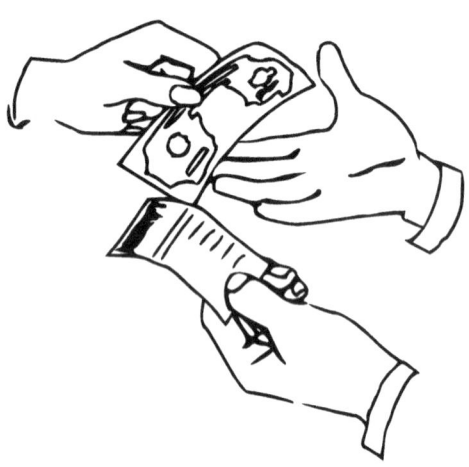

THE LIES

They're lying to you
When they say your words flow well
They're lying to you
When they say you'll be successful
They're lying to you
When they say you're important
They're lying to you
When they say you're unforgettable
They're lying to you
Because you are so much more than that

CLEAR VIEW

I wish to behold the power to transform
The world around us with words.
To take others to scenes
more beautiful than they imagined.
In astonishing ways
I want to change their view
to see the world as it is
not a world we pretend
to be perfect.

I've exhausted my hand
trying to create what
sounds right,
looks right,
is right,
according to the righteous
 standards of our society
But nothing is done well
Unless it feels right

I don't care how you read these poems.
Whether in one quick sitting
or by studying them for days on end.
I just want you to see that I believe in you
 and encourage you
to believe in yourself.
Fears are real and intimidating. Bleed and cry
Into your work. Make it
an important part of yourself.
A part of you that glows from within.

Just read them

To the one that feels lost
And has no plans for the future
I hope you find what makes you happy
I hope you find something to bring that
sparkle to your eyes
'Cause right now they're glazed over
with dread
I see how much you're fighting to get
out of this prison
'Cause the outside world is ugly too,
so please **stay**

To the one who isn't encouraged
to follow their heart. How foolish of them
to let their distorted view of art
guide the words they say to you.

To put every ounce of your being
into what you love and to be told
you won't make a career out of art.

To feel these pains
through every muscle and bone
in your fragile skin and to spend a multitude
of hours trying to prove them wrong.

To go above and beyond, you always have a place here
with me.

READING MEMORIES

Watching the sun rise and set like clockwork,
admiring the variety of colors each one brings

One day I will lose the strength to remember
the brushstrokes strewn into every unique sky

I'll keep my words to repaint those scenes
Reminding me of the beautiful life I have lived

NEW HOUSE

How exciting
To break open a new notebook
The silky
Texture of its empty pages
Enjoyed far
Beyond the tedious work that
Passes its
pages left each day eager
To be the
Next house of my thoughtless words

The wheel of time never stops turning
The system doesn't sleep
Only continues to bleach our minds
and rob us of our creative potential
We must rejoice
For this structured time is our only hope

Every experience is a star.
Some burn bright and hot
Gone in a moment's time.
Others burn long and furiously,
When you look at them all lit
At once, the connections begin
to form the **constellations** of
our lives.

Having access
To this inspiring world fuels my desires
To be fulfilled with the utmost precision
I can muster
Art is the greatest **tribute** we can give back

STAMPS

Stamp on my forehead
I should be excluded
And watch in disillusion
as I feel no pain
From those
I will eventually
pass by
without
thinking
twice.

After years of being left behind
It finally does not phase me
To not be chased
or sought after
I am fine doing things on my own
There is no point in being present
If I am not
Wanted
So go ahead, **pass me by**
I will let out a sigh of relief
Knowing I am better off

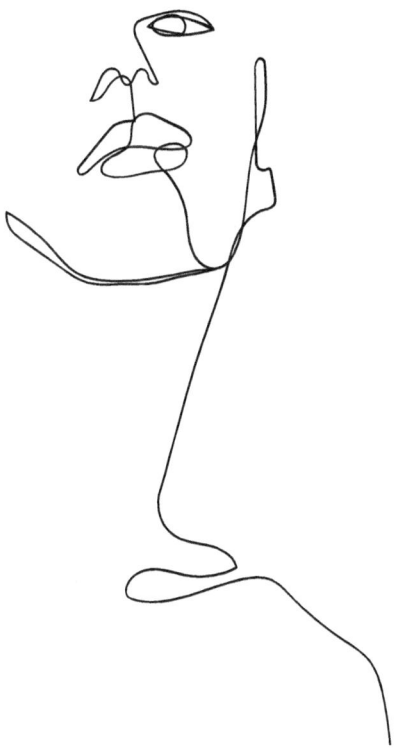

www.ingramcontent.com/pod-product-compliance
Lightning Source LLC
Chambersburg PA
CBHW071122160426
43196CB00013B/2673